Copyrighted Material

This book or parts thereof may not be reproduced in any form whatsoever, store or transmitted by any means-electronic, photocopy, mechanical recording or otherwise without prior permission of the publisher.

Copyright @2020 by Walter Abraham

All right reserved

Table of contents

How to get started in the stock market	4
Stock market explained	5
Investment basics in stocks	6
Purpose of stock market	7
Why are shares traded?	9
What is a stock symbol?	17
What is a stock trend?	18
Stocks appreciation	19
Dividend Earnings	20
What's the cost of a share?	21
Recessions and bear market	23
What causes recessions?	24
Stock terminology every investor must know	26

Tips for stocks investment for beginners   37

HOW TO GET STARTED IN THE STOCK MARKET

The first step in getting started in the stock market is to save up some capital and determine how much you could invest in stock from your saving. You need to have spare money you don't need for the foreseeable future to invest in stock. The volume of stocks you are able to buy depends on the level of your savings and the amount you are willing to invest in those stocks.

To be able to buy the real stocks, you need to engage the service of a stock broker or a stock fund provider. You can't go the stock exchange market yourself as an individual to buy shares. You need the services of a broker who facilitate the buying of stocks on your behalf. You broker can be your bank or financial institution providing broker services. Take note that for every stock you buy, the broker will take a small fee known as ''brokerage''.

It actually costs money to invest in stocks, so it's advisable to keep your stock buying to a minimum level and be decisive in your investment, this way you can keep your transaction costs low. Many people, especially beginners tend to lose large chunk of their profits to costs.

The next thing is to be patient and not to be in a rush to sell off your stocks. Hold on to your stocks as long as possible. The holding window period is actually where your profits lie. The more you hold on to your stocks the more the chances of it appreciating and increasing in value and volumes. Also, you keep the costs low this way and you don't lose money unnecessarily.

STOCK MARKET EXPLAINED

People often look at stock market as a place to put their money and reap profits without actually understands what stock market is all about. Yes, it is true that you could create wealth and financial independence by investing in stock market but the question is what is stock market and does it operates?

In a simple term, stock market is a global network market where securities are traded for money. Shares are security and it is a portion of a company. When a share is being bought, it means one is buying a small ownership of that company. So in a nutshell, stock market is a market where company shares are being traded i.e. bought and sold.

INVESTMENT BASICS IN STOCKS

Investment learning can be likened to learning how to ride a bike. The task will look difficult at first but with constant practice, you will get use to it and will be able to ride freely. The truth is that, while learning bike's riding does not guarantee you a top spot, it can get you to your destination a bit easier and faster. So, learning about the basic in investment in stock can actually help you in minimizing the risks and mistakes often made in the stocks market by people especially the beginners.

A stock can be said to be a partial ownership of a company by investors i.e. as an investor, when you buy a share of a company, you owe a small fraction of that company's assets and this gives you a claim over its future earnings.

As an investor, you can make money from stock investment through two basic ways. The first way is through stock appreciation and the second is through a dividend citation earnings.

PURPOSE OF THE STOCK MARKET
What is the purpose of the stock exchanges and why do they exist? If you think about it, as companies begin to grow frequently they need

more cash to build a new manufacturing facility or even to buy a competitor and one of the ways that they can do that is by selling stock in their company. Now could they go out and sell that stock directly to you? Yes they can, most private companies in the United States certainly do it that way.

However a great number of companies have decided to sell their stock publicly and then list those share prices on newspapers and websites so that their employees and the current shareholders can see how they're doing. It's a way to raise capital so that they then have more cash to go and buy or build whatever their projects are, that they feel will benefit their company for the long term, so that's why they exist.

In a normal market, goods can be touched and taken home but on the stock market, only virtual goods in the form of stocks are traded. They are listed in the form of share prices which can appreciate or depreciate within seconds. Investors therefore have to react swiftly in taking decision in order not to miss out on opportunity. A simple rumor can influence the rise and demand for a share company's shares and the same rumor can lead to its decline in shares. So the stock market provides an opportunity for company to list their shares for members of the public. It also avail members of the public opportunity to see shares listed before making an investment decisions.

WHY ARE SHARES TRADED?

Capital is needed to build a large company and this can be raised by way of selling shares. Company typically raised capital to grow and expand their business through shares sales. This can be done by an initial public offering or IPO. The IPO is a process when portion of company's shares is being sold to public investors.

When company goes public, its stocks are opened to the members of the public to be bought. So, there is a need for market place for company to trade their securities and this market place is known as stock exchange.

There are various stock exchanges around the world where stocks are traded on daily basis. There is New York stock Exchange in the U.S, NSE in India, JPX in Japan, TSX in Canada and among others. These stocks are global in nature where shares are traded all over the world. The stock exchange allows companies to raise capital to continue their growth and expansion.

For instance, facebook sold over $400 million shares in its initial public offer at $38 per share and over $16 billion was raised through this offer from investors. Share value is the representative of company in stock market and its shows well a company is doing in business and as company grow so does its shares in the stock market. This also portray a good sign for investor because as the company experience growth in value so does the investors' original investment in the company. Sometimes company's shares appreciate in value to the extent that the unit shares multiply (through share bonus) and get so expensive, this is when stock splits occur. For instance, 10 unit shares of Apple after their IPO in 1980 is now presently worth 560 shares.

For example, let's say you took your company public with 100 shares and you decided to sell 50 of these shares for $100 each as your initial public offering but now your company has grown significantly and your shares are now worth $500 each. The average investor is no longer able to afford to buy your stock. So to make sure your shares are easier for the public to buy, you do a two-for-one split which means that each share splits into two shares. Now instead of having 100 shares in your company, your company now has 200 total shares.

Share splitting can also be explained as splitting the value of the original share into two. Take $200 shares as example, after a two-to-one split, that shares are now two shares worth $100 each. This motivates investors to invest in your stock and continue investing in your company. This equally means that any investors with initial 5 unit stocks in your company before the split now have 10 unit stocks and the value of their investment. For example, Apple shares were $22 per share in 1980 during their initial public offering. The first two-to-one split of Apple happened in 1987 when the stock rose to $79 per share, reducing the share price by half i.e. $39.50 means that your 5 shares bought during the initial public offering is now 10 Apple shares.

In the year 2000, Apple had her second two-to-one split when the stock was trading at $111 per share. This means that your initial 5 shares purchased during the IPO are now 20 shares.

The third two-to-one split of Apple happened in 2005 when the stock witnessed a decline, trading at $90 per share. Apple share price dropped down to $45 per share and this will also affect your shares volume, meaning that your initial 5 shares are now 40 shares at $45 each.

In 2014, Apple stock rose to $656 per share and the company had a massive 7 to 1 split of their stock. This means your original 5 unit shares during the IPO now become 280 shares worth $93.71 cents per share. Apple stock finished year 2019 with $293.65 per share and by February 2020 before the global lockdown, Apple share price was value at $327 per share.

Sometimes stock price don't reflect the company's true state as negative rumor can crash the value of the company's shares in the market, which can terribly affect its business performance. Positive rumor can as well positively boost the company's shares value and as well as its market performance. Investors can invest in company's shares if they see value in it. Another thing that can influence investors into buying company's shares is the potential idea behind the company itself, the more the investors sees great potential behind the idea of the company the more he'll be willing to invest in the company.

Young company can actually attract investors in raising capital for their businesses not minding their current state i.e. they may actually be losing money at that moment. A good example is the Snapchat, the social media platform who was able to raise more than $3billion through the initial public offer despite not being profitable before doing the IPO.

Company can use the capital generated from the sales of its shares to members of the public to transform their idea to reality and begin making profits from it. In an extreme bad case, the company can run out of capital before becoming profitable which will lead to investors losing the capital invested in the company. Company's worth can run into billions on paper because of speculation generated by financial bubble where the company's stock price is not the practical value of the company. This can results into the loss of capital invested by investors. This was a situation in the United States in 2001when internet was a new trend and many internet companies were just starting up. Many investors in anticipation of good returns invested lots of capital into the shares of these companies at high price with expectation that those shares will grow in value, but this never happened as most of those companies failed to turned profit. Most of those shares were later sold at a loss by investors.

Many factors influence the share prices; one of such is the company's image. Another is the supply and demand of the company's shares in stock market which results in daily fluctuation of share prices. This is the major reason why stock expert recommended portfolio investment diversification as well as long term investment. It's worth mentioning that stock market also has both expansions and recessions period.

A company can raise funds by selling its shares to finance expansion of its business. Sometimes shares trading can be said to be a game of chance because nobody can accurately say which company will perform well and which will not. Though, a company with good reputation is likely to be back by investors, likewise the opposite for a company with a bad reputation.

WHAT IS A STOCK SYMBOL?

Do you own stock in coca-cola or Pepsi or McDonald's or GE or Unilever or Chevron or BP and on and on and on do you ever wonder how to identify your company if you look it up in the newspaper or look it up on a website.

The way to identify stock on exchange is through stock symbols, meaning each company has chosen a group of letters to help identify the shares sold by that company on specific exchanges. For instance, in Hong Kong everything is in numbers, but on the Nasdaq in the United States there are four letters. So it really depends upon the country and the exchange that you're dealing with but the key is, each individual will have an ID and you need to understand what that ID is in order to figure out what the value of your holdings are.

WHAT IS A STOCK TREND?

I have a friend who writes down prices of stocks every day in a notebook and that's the way he tracks the trend in the share price. Trend might mean the price is moving up or down. A trend is the difference between two prices and some people think this happens over a very long term. The truth is that this movement can happen in seconds, minute even days.

One way to identify stock trends is to go on the website of the stock brokerage firm or even Google stock trend. If you Google, you'll see a list of companies and you can look through them to determine if there are companies out there that have the characteristics that you like.

Another way to monitor trend is to look at the back of business magazines and business newspapers, there are charts but though that chart list is not going to be anything of comprehensive as they are limited by the number of pages in the publication. You're probably better off using a technical trading software package that you could buy or use in order to identify companies that are either moving up or moving down in price.

STOCK APPRECIATION:

Stock appreciation is a situation where your stock increases in value. For example, as an investor, if you purchase a stock of Coca Cola at $1 and after sometimes the price goes up to $2. You could then sell the stock to another investor at $2 per share and you make profit. Suppose you invest $5,000 in purchasing the shares of Coca Cola, at $1 per shares. The stock appreciation of Coca cola from $1 to $2 wills double the worth of your investment from $5,000 to $10,000. So, if you decide to sell the whole of your 5,000 units share bought at $1 per share. You'll make $10,000 and a profit of $5,000.

DIVIDEND EARNINGS:

You can also make money from stock through dividend earning. Company gives portion of their earnings to shareholders periodically. Thus, dividend earnings are a periodic payment issued to shareholders by company. The amount you earn on stock depends on the volume and value of your stock.

Let's use a typical example here. Suppose we have a company known as Blue moon that produces paint. The company is so good that that it witness high patronage and this prompted the management to think of expansion. The company will need to raise capital to achieve this expansion plan. One of the ways to raise this capital is by taking loan, which would mean taking a significant amount of debts. Another way is to issue shares of stock to members of the public. By issuing stock to public, the company can raise the needed capital without running into debts. This would mean, the company will sell small ownership to investors and the investors will have a claim on future earnings of the company.

An investor with extra cash looking for an investment with potential for better returns will see Blue moon as promising company with potential of growth would then buy its stock. The capital realizes from the sales of this stock is what Blue moon company will plough back into the business for expansion.

WHAT'S THE COST OF A SHARE?
If a company like Blue moon decide to raise a share of $2,000,000 at the Initial Public Offering (IPO) and decides to issue out 2,000 shares of

stock. Each share qualifies as a little fraction of the company's worth and each share would be value at $2,000 as the initial market price.

Suppose, after the IPO the share price remain the same and an investor purchases a single share of $2,000 in the open market. What are the likely things that can happen to his investment?

In a situation where the company enjoy business boost with high patronage, its stock price may appreciate. If this happens, the investor could turn profit by selling off his shares to another investor. On the other hand, if there is downturn in the business and the company's stock witnessed a decline in value, the investor could lose his money if he decides to sell off his share at this point.

Therefore, in stock market investment, the basic goal is to invest in stock when the prices depreciate and sell when the prices appreciate.

Stock are consider volatile investment compare to other investment option like bond because sometimes the price changes quickly and a times remains same for a long time. However, the stock market will continue to remain attractive to investor because its increased risk comes with potential for greater returns.

RECESSIONS AND BEAR MARKETS

People often equate recessions with bear markets and some even believe that they're the same thing or happened at the same time. In actual fact, recessions and bear markets are two different things. So what's the difference?

According to the National Bureau of Economic Research, ''recession is a decline in an economic lasting more than a few months as measured by indices like, workers' income, rates of employment, gross domestic product, retail sales and manufacturing output''.

What causes recession?
Recession is largely caused by big declines in consumer spending. In the United States, consumers' spending comprises 70% of the economy. The big declines in the consumer spending mostly lead to shocks to the system. The shock can be an internal like the tech bubble that was witnessed in 2000 or the great financial crisis that happened in 2008. The shock can also be an external shock like the pandemic we're experiencing now.

Economic recessions and expansions are nothing extra ordinary, they are part of a normal cycle, that's something that happens and to be remembered. There have been about 12 recessions since 1945 occurring every 5 years. These recessions lasts on average of less than 12 months. An expansion on the other hand typically lasts much longer, sometimes more than four years on average.

The bear market:

A bear market can be defined as a declined in the stock market by more than 20%. This is usually associated with widespread pessimism and negative investor sentiment.

Going by our definition of recession at bear markets, we need to put it at heart that the economy differs from stock market and recessions and bear market are also not the same. Recessions shows great economic decline while the bear markets reflect significant declines in the stock market. So, bear markets and recessions and don't always happen at the same time.

There is an imperfect connection between recessions and bear markets. The key factor about the duo is that stocks tend to appreciate in value after a bear market and before recession ends. Thus, as a result of this imperfect connection, we can rightly predict what'll happen in the short term.

To recap, recession and bear markets differ, they are not the same and they don't always occur at the same time. Stocks' movement tends to be upward in direction over the long term especially towards the end of recession. Your investment strategy should be a function of your time horizon and your personal circumstances, not the current events.

STOCK MARKET TERMINOLOGY EVERY TRADER MUST KNOW

It is very frustrating when you hear someone talking with passion about stock market and financials and things related to this sector and some people are confused. This is even more frustrating especially if the speaker does not know how to communicate with regular people that has no background knowledge of stock market. Stock market just like many other area of business is full of terminology jargons which may be confusing to a newbie. This section shed light and explains some of those terminologies.

TICKER SYMBOLS:

Sometimes you hear someone say ''hey what's a ticker symbol for that stock?''. Every stock that trades in market has a specific ticker symbol that you can look up to see its stock price i.e. the symbol that it trades under as a stock. For instance, Apple doesn't trade under Apple, it trades under AAPL. So the ticker symbol for Apple is ''AAPL''. So, if you want to go on Yahoo Finance and look up Apple's stock price and as financials, you type in AAPL and then all that will pull up.

Pandora, the internet streaming service ticker symbol is P and AXP for America Express Company. When you go public as a company you get to pick what your ticker symbol is going to be as long as it's something that hasn't already been taken on the NASDAQ exchange or the NYSC or whatever exchange. So, that's what a ticker symbol means.

ONLINE BROKERAGE:

When you hear people say set up an online brokerage account or people ask how you invest in stock. You need to set up an online brokerage account. what that is it's like Scottrade, etrade, TD Ameritrade a lot of those services they're what's called online brokerages and you make an account with them and you can funnel money through your bank account into those accounts and you can actually invest in a stock or a bond or whatever it is you're trying to invest in that's what an online brokerage is

BULL MARKET:

What's a bull market? What a bull market means is stocks are going up, that means the whole markets doing great that's what they call a bull market. When the stocks are going to the moon i.e. bull market. I'm bullish on this stock what does that mean that means? I believe that stocks going up a bullish a bowl **mean a stock markets going up,** it's off on bullish on a stock I believe a particular stock is going up.

BEAR MARKET:

Bear market what's a bear market? You hear people say oh that's a bear market right now. You don't want to invest the bear markets when stocks are going down, that's a bear market. If I say I'm bearish on a stock bear means what bearish market means the whole markets going down. So, if I'm bearish on a stock it means I believe a particular stock is going down. So bull market good thing bear market not a good thing.

HOLD:
it's a hold you hear people say oh that stock gets a hold what that means is if you're a new investor in that stock you don't buy it, but if you're already invested in that stock to hold it that you want to hold it right now. So, if you haven't invested don't jump in now, but if you are already holding the shares you hold it.

LONG:
This term is often used with the opposite word ''short'' and it simply means a particular direction of an event. For instance, when you heard trader

says "I'm long" it means he'll make profit when the stock price appreciate.

For example, let's say someone says I'm long Amazon shares $50, it means he buy Amazon shares at 50 dollars and if Amazon share appreciate in value up to a 60 dollars, that's a profit of $10 per share, so that is what it mean by going long.

I'm a long here people all the time say I'm long this stock. What does that mean? That means you're in that stock for the long term you want to be a long term investor in that company so you're not looking at trade, you're not looking to sell it real quick. None of those kinds of things, you're long at that stock and you believe in it, in its future that it's going to do great.

SHORT:

When the trader is short, then he has to borrow shares from the stock broker to cover up. For example, assuming I'm short Amazon shares of $100 and I'm going to borrow $100 worth of shares from my broker. i.e. S100 worth of shares will be borrowed and let's say the stock price of Amazon goes down to $90, that mean I'll return back the Amazon shares because I bought one share of Amazon to return back this ten share.

I'm short that stock, what's that mean? that means you're a short seller, that stock you believe that stock is going down over time doesn't necessarily mean you believe it's going down to a long term but it means you believe it's going down at some point. Whether it's in a short term or long term that means I'm short, I think that stocks going down.

So let's say I buy this one share of Amazon at the open market for $90 and I return it back to my broker so in this case or in this example you can see that after the transaction is completed I borrow the shares and I return back the share at the end of the day. At the end of the day I made a profit of $10 per share, this is how short-selling works. You borrow the shares, you sell it at the market then you collect the proceeds, although you will release it right because they did. The broker will manage all this transaction right and once you buy back the shares, everything return back to your broker you would then know the difference. In this case since the stock price goes down, you make a profit of ten dollars. What about if stock price goes up? It moves against you, you make loss.

Let's see another example again. You short hundred dollars worth of Amazon shares and it moves up to $200, this means you collect hundred dollars upfront by borrowing the shares of Amazon and then when you need to pay back the shares of Amazon you buy it in the open market for $200. You can see that this is a loss of a hundred dollars to you because the price of the stock was against you, it went up higher.

So, one thing about short selling is that your losses is technically unlimited because if the share price of Amazon moves up to $5000, you can see that your losses can exceed your initial deposit, though short selling is not very common.

BID AND ASK:

Bid and ask, what is it all about?

There is no one price in the stock trading market and there are basically two key prices to pay attention to i.e. the bid and the ask price. The bid is the price you sell, if you want to sell a stock while the ask price is the price you pay if you want to buy the stock.

So, there's always two prices in the market, the ask price and the bid price. The **ask** price is the price you pay if you want to buy the stock, the bid price on the other hand is the price that you sell, if you want to sell a stock.

In other words, you have to look at the price if you are buying the stock because that's the price you have to pay. On the other hand, if you want to, you'll have to pay attention to the bid price because that is the price you sell.

SPREAD:

What does spread mean? Spread is the difference between the bids and asks. Let's explain this with some illustration. Supposing the asking price for

Amazon stock is $110 and the bid price is $100. The spread between this price is $10 i.e. the difference between the **"ask"** and **"bid"** and that is a transaction cost to you.

Transaction cost is the cost that you incur in the course of the transaction. If you buy Amazon shares at this time, you have to pay $110 and assuming you are ready to sell it immediately and you are able to sell it at $100, that is immediate loss of $10 to you and that's the spread you have to pay, this asides other commission and fees to the exchange. One important thing to note here is that large cap stocks are more liquid and you can actually expect a little spread.

TIPS FOR STOCKS INVESTMENT FOR BEGINNERS

Number one tip:

Beware of being caught in price movement:

Concentrate on the long term plan of your chosen stock and do not be distracted by the day to day stock price movement. Stock market investors, especially the beginners often get distracted by the stock price movement. This happen most often in the very first few month of their investment. The day to day price movement often leads these investors to get too high or too low on confidence. Suppose you invest $2,000 in stock and in a couple of months it depreciated in value by 10% and your $2,000 invested crashed to $1,800. Many investors would unhappy at this point and some may even sell off the stock for fear of further depreciation. Same thing apply to when the stock appreciates in value, they get high on confidence and think that they are genius in stock choice. So know that there will always be movement in the stock price. Avoid getting caught in the day-to-day stock price movement, have vision and focus on long term.

Number two tips:
Don't be emotional over stock:
Avoid getting too emotional with stock. Beginners often make mistake of falling in love with particular stock, even the advanced investors are guilty of this too. They get too emotional if somebody says something negative about the stock they love. They see other people's opinion concerning the stock they are in love as baseless. Remember that it's not your company and stock is just a way of making money.

Number three tips:
Invest in companies with strong balance sheet:
Target your investment in companies with strong balance sheet. Identify and invest in companies

that have the following indices; rich in cash, rich in short-term and long-term investments, have low short-term and long-term debts. This is a wise thing to do as a beginner in the stock market as you might not know how to predict future earnings yet.

The reason behind the choice of these indices is that suppose the companies have a rough time, their strong balance will be a leverage to withstand the storm unlike companies with a weak balance sheet that may likely keep accruing piles and piles of debt and might even face bankruptcy with little or no money coming in.

Number four tips:
Concentrate on your game and not others games: Never focus too much of your attention on how someone's return are going rather concentrate on your own effort. Focusing on someone result might put unnecessary pressure on you to perform or

want to perform more than that person, this might be counter-productive at the end of the day, you might lose focus. You are in the stock market to make money and not to compete with people. Your absolute focus should be to try to do better than the stock market does.

Number five tips:
Invest in companies you fully understand:
Avoid investing in companies you don't fully understand. Study and understand the companies you are investing your money in prior to your investment. You might find it pretty hard to understand the financials and other indices of companies you don't understand and this is like gambling. Your may have a better understanding of service industries than oil and gas companies, so investing in service industries' stock gives you a better understanding of what you are doing.

Number six tips:

Invest slowly in stocks market:

Some many beginners in stock market rush in putting a lot of money in stock at once. The fact that you have been researching stocks for weeks and watching videos on stock are not enough to rush in investing all of your savings in stocks at once. Never rush your investment in stocks. Supposed you have $5,000 you intend to invest overtime, spread your investment timing. Invest $1,000 at first and after few months invest another $1,000. After you have seen how your initial investment is fairing and you are confidence of your stocks performance, you can invest another $2,000 and so on. You are encourage to invest in the market but don't rush in doing this because you are still learning.

Number seven tips:

Start with one stock portfolio:

Portfolio diversification is good but don't rush into this as beginners. Start with buying one stock because your investment is small and starting with one stock portfolio will gives you the opportunity to focus on that one company and understand its earnings and market price movements over the months. Meanwhile, you can still go ahead and research other stocks but focus your investment on that one stock first and keep investing in it periodically. After sometimes, you could then go ahead and buy a second stock and then start adding a portfolio and maybe in a year and a half in the market, your portfolio must have grown to 3, 5 or 10 stocks. So, start with just one stock and then add another and then another, go like that till you gradually build your portfolio.

www.ingramcontent.com/pod-product-compliance
Lightning Source LLC
Chambersburg PA
CBHW072237230526
45466CB00024B/2090